S0-BDR-435

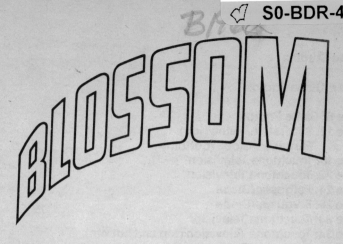

By
Lee Kilduff

Incorporated

Photo Credits:

Cover: Globe Photos

Page 6: Globe Photos
Page 12: Silverstein/Retna (top)
Ferguson/Globe (bottom)
Page 18: Touchtone Television
Page 22: Touchtone Television
Page 24: Ferguson/Globe
Page 26: Ferguson/Globe
Page 30: Touchtone Television
Page 34: Touchtone Television (top and bottom)
Page 38: Ferguson/Globe
Page 42: Barr/Retna
Page 46: Ferguson/Globe
Page 48: Touchtone Television
Page 52: Ferguson/Globe
Page 56: Touchtone Television
Page 62: Touchtone Television

Copyright © 1992 Kidsbooks, Inc.
7004 N. California Avenue
Chicago, IL 60645

ISBN: 1-56156-167-3

**All rights reserved including the right of reproduction
in whole or in part in any form.**

Manufactured in the United States of America

TABLE OF CONTENTS

Introduction

Do you tune in every week to find out what outrageous new situation Blossom and the gang have gotten themselves into? Do you call your friends after every episode to talk about Blossom's funky wardrobe? Do you want to know *everything* about Mayim Bialik—the cool, young celeb that brings Blossom to life?

Read on, because this book will answer all your questions about Mayim and the entire *Blossom* cast, including hot new heartthrob Joey Lawrence.

You'll find out why thousands of teens across the country relate to *Blossom*. You'll learn all about the "Blossom look."

And, by the time you finish this book, you'll be a Mayim maven!

The *Blossom* cast (clockwise from upper left): Buzz Richman [Barnard Hughes], Nick Russo [Ted Wass], Anthony Russo [Michael Stoyanov], Joey Russo [Joey Lawrence], Blossom Russo [Mayim Bialik] and Six LeMuere [Jenna von Oy].

CHAPTER ONE

Mayim's Early Days

Mayim Bialik never imagined she'd be starring in her own television show by the time she was 16. But she has dreamed of being an actress for as long as she can remember.

Mayim was born in San Diego, California, on December 12, 1975. Her parents named her Mayim, which means *water* in Hebrew, after her great-grandmother.

She and her older brother, Isaac, grew up in Los Angeles. When Mayim turned six, she announced to her parents that she wanted to be an actress. Mayim's parents, however, had other ideas.

"My parents really didn't want me to act," Mayim recalls with a laugh, "and they tried to discourage me."

Young Mayim thought acting seemed glamorous and fun. But her parents, Beverly and Barry Bialik, knew there was another side to show business.

Barry, who is a drama coach, and Beverly, a former filmmaker, knew show business could be tough and very cold. Actors and actresses are rejected for parts all the time. Beverly and Barry wanted to spare their daughter from that pain for as long as they could. Besides, they knew that parents of child stars often have to give up a great deal of time to watch over their children's careers, and they didn't want Isaac to feel left out.

Mayim listened to her parents, but she didn't give up on her dream. She just waited.

Mayim had started to learn ballet when she was four. When she was six, she started piano lessons and showed a flair for music. She began playing the trumpet when she was 10 and somehow found time to squeeze in jazz dancing. Although she also wanted to learn the trombone, Mayim couldn't.

"My arms were too short," Mayim says.

Any time she got the chance, Mayim volunteered to sing or act in school plays. It didn't take her teachers long to figure out how good she was! And it didn't take Mayim long to realize that acting wouldn't be a passing fancy.

At home, no one was safe from Mayim's impressions. She was always imitating someone or just cutting up.

"She's always been very funny," Beverly says.

Won over by their daughter's perseverance

and the incredible promise she showed, Beverly and Barry gave in to Mayim's wishes. When Mayim turned 11, her parents decided she was mature enough to understand that rejection was simply part of the business.

"We felt she was old enough and had enough self-esteem to understand what it means when people in this business don't want you," says Beverly. And, because Beverly had just stopped teaching nursery school, she knew she would have enough time to help Mayim get her best shot.

Beverly and Barry immediately became Mayim's biggest supporters. Beverly knew Mayim would need an agent if she was to become a success. So, she set about getting her the best one she could find.

Although she wasn't drop-dead gorgeous, young Mayim had engaging, offbeat looks. In the letters she sent to agents, Beverly described her daughter as a "Barbra Streisand-Bette Midler type of kid." Little did she guess that Mayim's biggest break would come when she played a child version of Bette Midler's character in the hit movie, *Beaches*!

Almost as soon as she got an agent, Mayim began working. She made guest appearances on shows such as *MacGyver* and *Webster*. She landed a small part in the horror flick *Pumpkinhead*. In *Pumpkinhead*, Lance Henricksen, of *Aliens* fame, stars as a father who convinces a witch to call down demons on a group of teens he mistakenly thinks were involved in his son's death.

"I got to scream a lot," Mayim says.

Even before that movie was released, however, Mayim got the phone call that would change her life. Mayim's agent told her to get ready to audition for a movie called *Beaches*.

CHAPTER TWO

Beaches

In *Beaches*, Mayim is such a perfect ringer for the brassy, wisecracking Bette Midler that it's hard to imagine anyone else playing the young C.C. Bloom. But Mayim wasn't handed the part. She worked hard for it.

When Mayim's parents were making movies during the 1960s, they filmed Bette Midler performing in New York City. Mayim studied this video before trying out.

"It gave me an idea of what she was like," Mayim says. However, Mayim wasn't really convinced that she had a good shot at getting the role. After all, Bette Midler is a brown-eyed redhead. Mayim has green eyes and brown hair.

But Mayim being Mayim, she showed up for the first audition sporting a flaming red wig and a sassy, brassy walk. Although scores of other Midler

Child actress
Mayim Bialik
gets her break
portraying a
spunky young
Bette Midler
in the hit
movie *Beaches.*

Mayim gets
strong support from
her biggest fans...
Mom and Dad.

look-alikes auditioned and wanted the part as badly as she did, something about Mayim's style caught director Garry Marshall's eye.

"Mayim was shy at first," Marshall recalls. "But the second time we saw her, she was cooking." And, through the auditions that followed, she never stopped cooking. At the final audition, Mayim tried out one last time with Bette Midler watching. When the audition was over, Mayim hoped she had impressed Bette. But Mayim wasn't sure if she had won the part.

"She's very quiet in person," Mayim says of Bette, "so I didn't really have a clue whether she liked me." Mayim needn't have worried. A day later, Mayim received that long-awaited phone call. She was asked to appear in *Beaches*.

In the movie, Mayim and Bette play C.C. Bloom, a Brooklyn kid who becomes a big entertainer. The movie centers around a special friendship between C.C. and Hillary Essex, who is played by Barbara Hershey. C.C. and Hillary remain friends as they grow up and go their separate ways. Although their friendship is sometimes rocky, it's C.C. who comes through when Hillary gets sick and needs her.

Mayim plays C.C. at age 11, when she first meets Hillary on the Atlantic City boardwalk. Dressed in a satin bodysuit, black fishnet stockings, and a feather boa, Mayim looks just like you would imagine Bette looking at the same age. Whether she's tap-dancing her heart out or lounging on the boardwalk cracking jokes, Mayim captures Bette's style.

When Mayim was rehearsing, however, she never tried to sound like Bette. "I didn't really think of it as playing Bette Midler, which made it easier," Mayim recalls. "I got the lines. I read them and that was it." The hardest part about learning the part was when Bette personally taught Mayim the dance steps.

"I didn't want her to think I was some *schlock*," says Mayim, using a Yiddish expression for something that's shoddy. Mayim had no need to worry. When the movie came out, no one thought Mayim was a *schlock*. Everyone thought she was pretty special. Film critics called Mayim "amazing" and "irresistible."

Audiences loved the movie, an old-fashioned tear-jerker packed with laughter, songs, fights, and reunions. When Mayim came on the screen, movie-goers *oohed* and *aahed* at her talent and her resemblance to Bette Midler. One critic even told readers to see *Beaches* for the "mind-boggling performance of look-alike Mayim Bialik."

Only Mayim failed to see the resemblance between herself and Bette. "People said I looked a lot like Bette," recalls Mayim, "but I didn't see it. Afterward, people kept saying it, but I still didn't see it."

One thing that everyone, including Bette, did see was that Mayim had a special talent for acting. At a cast party held when the movie was completed, Bette said that Mayim had a very bright future in acting. And what a future it would be!

Talk show hosts all across the country invited

Mayim to come talk about *Beaches* on TV. All the attention surprised Mayim.

"I was aware there was a lot of positive feedback from the movie," remembers Mayim, "but I was caught off guard. When I did that movie, I knew it was a great opportunity, but I didn't think of it as the thing that was going to make my career."

Movie and television offers poured in. Mayim soon was appearing on many popular shows. She landed a recurring role on *The Facts of Life* and guest-starred on *Doogie Howser, M.D.* She even played a young version of Murphy Brown on the hit show that stars Candice Bergen.

It was an exciting time for Mayim. While her parents kept her down-to-earth at home with such chores as cleaning her room, dusting the furniture, and helping with the ironing, writers in Hollywood were creating parts with Mayim in mind.

In the summer of 1990, Mayim starred in a Fox sitcom called *Molloy*. Mayim played Molloy, a street-smart Manhattan teenager who moves to Beverly Hills after her dad remarries. In the show, she acts in a children's series while trying to adjust to her new family, including her snobby older stepsister.

Although the critics loved Mayim's spunky performance, they were less kind to the show, and it was canceled after about six episodes.

After that, Mayim was offered parts on the TV series *Life Goes On* and in the movie *Troop Beverly Hills*. But Mayim's agent thought she should wait for another starring role. Mayim listened to her agent.

"My parents trust my agent," Mayim says, "and I trust my parents."

Luckily, her agent was right and Mayim didn't have to wait long. Her life was about to "blossom" big time!

CHAPTER THREE

Mayim "Blossoms"

Try to imagine the *Blossom* show—only with a boy as the main character. Ridiculous, right? Yet that's just what almost happened.

The show's creator and producer, Don Reo, originally based *Blossom* on the life of a musician friend and his son.

"Initially the show focused on the boy, and Blossom was his younger sister," Reo says.

But as people at the NBC network worked on developing the show, they realized there were already several great shows centered around adolescent boys, including *The Wonder Years* and *Doogie Howser, M.D.* NBC and Reo decided to make Blossom the center of their new show.

Once that decision was made, finding a young celeb to star as Blossom was easy. Reo immediately

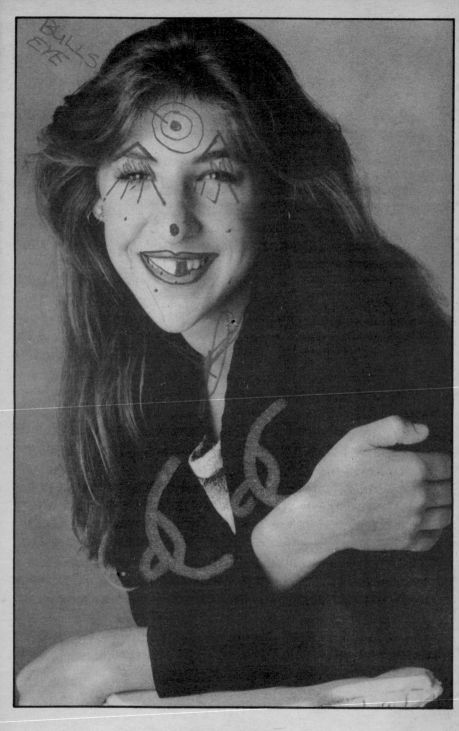

Mayim Bialik,
Blossom's **bright and beautiful star.**

thought of Mayim. He knew she was bright, funny, and loaded with talent.

"There are a lot of kids in this town who are actors," Reo says, "but there are very few who have the kind of gift she has. She knows how to deliver a line without being told how. She somehow just knows."

Because Reo has a daughter, he found it easy to build a new show around Blossom—especially once he knew she would be played by Mayim. Reo also hired several female writers to work on the show.

In the sitcom, Mayim stars as Blossom Russo, a teenage girl who is growing up in an otherwise all-male household.

Blossom's family consists of her musician dad, Nick; her 17-year-old brother, Joey, a not-too-bright, girl-crazed jock; and her older brother, Anthony, who's a paramedic.

Although Blossom's mother is away in Paris trying to make it as a singer, the Russo household gets plenty of visits from hip maternal grandfather Buzz Richman, a traveling musician who always has time for Blossom and her brothers.

With no older female role model in the house, Blossom is often left to her own devices as she learns what being a woman is all about. Luckily, Blossom's best friend and next-door neighbor, Six, is usually around to help. Together, the two deal with the many things that come up in any teenage girl's life.

On the show, Blossom has met her first real

boyfriend, Vinnie Bonitardi—played by David Lascher of *Beverly Hills, 90210* fame—and even experienced her first pangs of jealousy.

Mayim and Six also manage to pack in a lot of good times. In one episode, the pair sleep outside a concert hall to try to get tickets to a show by C&C Music Factory. At the end of the show, the girls are surprised when they actually meet and dance with the band members themselves!

Blossom has a lot of these unexpected moments, and Mayim thinks that's what helps to make the show so special. In another episode, for example, Blossom finds herself in the midst of a long music video.

"We don't want to fall into the trap of being a predictable show," Mayim says, "because that's what makes people tune out. We want to show people new stuff."

Whatever *Blossom* is doing does indeed work. The show has been a success with teenagers and is one of the hottest comedies on television. And Mayim is partly responsible for that!

She has a big part in almost every show, and she loves it. "I like to be busy," Mayim says. "I love to always be working and I like being in every scene."

Even though *Blossom* is a big hit, the show's young stars still have to go to school. The show is taped around Mayim and her co-stars' school day. There is a classroom right on the set where they are all tutored. In September 1992, Mayim started her senior year as a student in the Los

Angeles County High School's Independent Study Program.

With studying and rehearsing, putting on a hit show is a lot of work for Mayim and the gang. But the cast still manages to squeeze in some time for fun on the set.

On Mayim's 16th birthday, the cast surprised her with a party, complete with a birthday cake and a ton of fabulous gifts. The best present for Mayim —and almost any teenage girl—would have been a visit from Luke Perry and Jason Priestley. But the two hot Beverly Hills babes couldn't come by. So they sent over the next best thing—autographed photos.

The party turned into a real family affair. Mayim's parents came by. Joey Lawrence's brother Matthew, who tapes his show, *Walter and Emily*, on a nearby set, also shared the cake.

Mayim, Jenna, and the guys also like to fool around on the day they tape the show. They try to stick clothespins on people's backs without them noticing.

"We've gotten people so good," Jenna says. "One time I got someone's hair and they didn't even notice. It's really fun. We have a good time."

So if you ever see a clothespin dangling from Joey's sweat shirt, you'll know why!

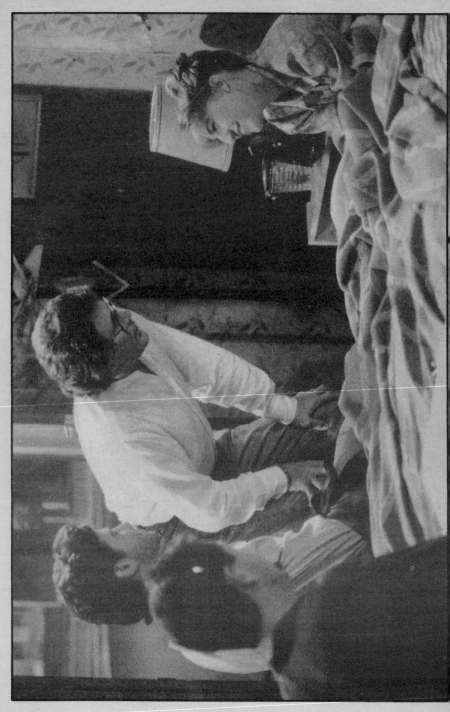

On the set, director Bill Bixby (yes, the Incredible Hulk!) gives last minute instructions to Blossom as David Lascher (left) looks on.

CHAPTER FOUR

All About Blossom

It's no secret that many teens think Blossom is cool. She seems like just the kind of kid you'd want for your best friend. She's smart, fun, confident, and acts like herself around guys.

Mayim likes Blossom that way. Ever since she took the part, Mayim has made sure Blossom doesn't act like an airhead.

"I didn't want my character to be the typical no brainer who is just interested in shopping and boys," Mayim says. "Basically, I want to break down the stereotypes."

Mayim has done just that. If she thinks Blossom isn't being treated properly by the writers, Mayim takes her objections to the producers. One time, Mayim objected to a script that poked fun at Blossom not getting dates because she was flat-chested. She got the script changed. Anoth-

Mayim makes sure that Blossom is portrayed as smart and sensible.

er time, Mayim didn't like a show that had Blossom shaving her legs.

"When it comes to things like that," Mayim says, "you don't have to go along. Especially with the flat-chested jokes. I think that's sexist. I think it's very insulting to me as a woman."

Mayim tries hard to make Blossom the kind of character you'd like to have around.

"I'm very happy that I'm in a position where I can show kids how to care and how to be a nice person," Mayim says. "I'm glad to have the responsibility of being looked up to."

Everyone always asks Mayim if she's like Blossom. You may wonder about that, too.

Mayim says she and Blossom are different in many ways. "Blossom is a lot more bubbly and enthusiastic," Mayim says. "Our musical tastes are different, and I think I am more sophisticated. Blossom is more the cheerleader type."

But there is one way that Blossom and Mayim are very much alike: They both love to shop.

One of Blossom's many looks!

CHAPTER FIVE

The Blossom Look

Even though Blossom has other things besides shopping on her mind, she does love her clothes. In fact, it's hard to say who likes clothes more, Blossom or Mayim! But their styles couldn't be more different.

On a typical episode, Blossom wears six different outfits . . . and they're all cool! The show's wardrobe people find Blossom's clothes the same way you find yours—by doing lots and lots of shopping. They spend many afternoons trekking all around Melrose Avenue, and stop in such Valley hangouts as The Limited. After they buy outfits for the show, however, the seamstresses often change the clothing before Blossom wears it. An outfit might be dyed, a funky trim might be sewn onto a vest, or a new dress might be created from parts of two others.

"Blossom is really wild," Mayim says. "But it's realistic fashion. It's not things that can't be found." A typical Blossom outfit could consist of leggings, suspenders, a flowered vest worn over a baggy shirt, and a funky hat.

Six's clothes, which are very Valley, are bought right from area stores and are almost never changed.

When Mayim and Jenna are away from the set, however, they have styles that are different from the characters they play.

Jenna thinks accessories can really make an outfit. She also pays a lot of attention to making sure her clothes work well together.

"It really annoys me when things clash," Jenna says, "when people wear stripes and flowers, or when their colors don't match."

Most often, Mayim reaches for jeans and a T-shirt or some baggy, black clothes. It's not that Mayim doesn't like the way Blossom dresses. She does. But Mayim thinks it's important to stay out of character when she's living her own life.

"I don't want to dress like the character," Mayim says, "because then when I go home, I'm not really me."

However, Mayim still loves seeing teens dress like Blossom. It's a good thing, too, because thousands of teens love to do just that!

CHAPTER SIX

The Co-Stars of Blossom

Mayim Bialik isn't the only reason *Blossom* is such a big hit. Joey Lawrence, Jenna von Oy, and the rest of the *Blossom* cast also have a lot to do with the show's success.

Blossom's brother, Joey Russo, is a popular jock who's more interested in scoring with the girls than in scoring high grades in school. Blossom thinks talking to Joey is a lot like talking to a hand puppet.

Joey Lawrence, 16, couldn't be more different. This hunky, brown-eyed babe is a high school honor student who excels in English literature, Latin, Greek, and French. And that's the way his mother likes it.

"My mom is really on top of the school thing and the homework thing," Joey says.

Hunky Joey (Joey Lawrence) is Blossom's brother, seventeen years old and crazy about girls.

Joey dreams of one day going to an Ivy League college such as Yale University.

"I'm going to make sure that I go to college," Joey says, "so that I have the information to be successful in other areas, if I have to."

Born in Philadelphia, Pennsylvania, Joey is the son of an insurance broker and a former school teacher. At age five, Joey had his picture taken by the studio staff at an East Coast department store. The photographer thought Joey was cute enough to turn professional.

He couldn't have been more right. At his first audition, Joey landed a role in a commercial. By age six, Joey had sung with Johnny Carson on *The Tonight Show*. After that, Joey won guest-starring roles on *Silver Spoons* and *Diff'rent Strokes*.

Before joining *Blossom*, Joey starred as Joey Donovan on the hit series *Gimme A Break*, which ran for six years. He's been featured in such movies as *Summer Rental*, *Hit & Run*, *Pulse*, and *Chains of Gold*.

Despite a hectic professional life, Joey has always found time for his many interests. He has run on his school's track team and played center field on the baseball team. Lately, he has been working out with a trainer to bulk up his hot bod.

These days, Joey splits his time between Los Angeles and his home in a Philadelphia suburb, where he lives with his parents and younger brothers, 11-year-old Matthew and five-year-old Andrew.

Joey is a major car fanatic. He loves antique

cars and has a huge model car collection. Not too long ago, Joey got his first real car, a Lexus.

When Joey's not hanging out on his bed reading car magazines, he likes to shoot pool with his friends, horse around with his brothers, and play video games.

Like almost everyone on the *Blossom* set, Joey is also musical. Two of his biggest passions are playing piano and writing his own songs.

"Music is probably the one thing I love more than cars," Joey says, "and sometimes more than acting, too."

Joey is so talented that the music industry has already noticed him. He recently recorded his debut R & B album, which features original songs. When Joey listens to other people's music, he reaches for discs by Johnny Gill, Bobby Brown, and Vanessa Williams.

Joey is not the only brother in Blossom's life. Michael Stoyanov stars as the oldest Russo brother, Anthony. Anthony is a recovering substance abuser who works as a paramedic. His family's support is important to him as he strives to remain sober.

In real life, Michael was born in Chicago, Illinois. He began his acting career in theater and has performed with the renowned Second City Theater.

Michael has made numerous appearances on television. He has guest-starred on *Empty Nest*, *Quantam Leap*, *Married . . . With Children*, *T.J. Hooker*, and *Crime Story*. He has also been featured in a number of made-for-television movies, including *Out on the Edge* and *Exile*.

On the big screen, Michael has appeared in *Nowhere to Run, Big Shots*, and *Mom and Dad Save the World*. Most recently, he played one half of a very unusual set of Siamese twins in the flick *Hideous Mutant Freakz*.

Like Joey Lawrence, Michael is an antique car nut. He also enjoys playing football, listening to opera, and winding down in the evening with his cat Mussolini and a good book.

Ted Wass stars as Nick, Blossom's dad and the head of the Russo household. A freelance studio musician, Nick is a single father trying his best to raise Blossom and her brothers without the help of their absent mother.

Ted Wass is probably best known for portraying Danny Dallas on the hit comedy series, *Soap*, although he does have a long list of other stage and film credits. Ted has appeared in such movies as *Curse of the Pink Panther, Oh God, You Devil*, and *The Long Shot*. On Broadway, Wass appeared in *Grease* and *They're Playing Our Song*.

Like the character he portrays, Wass has a love for music. A professionally trained opera singer, Ted also enjoys popular music. As a teen, he sang and played bass guitar for eight years with a rock 'n' roll band.

A native of Lakewood, Ohio, Ted got his start in show business at the Goodman Theater in Chicago, Illinois. He is married to actress Janet Margolin, and has a son Julian and a daughter Matilda.

Blossom with her TV dad (Ted Wass).

Anthony, played by Michael Stoyanov, is Blossom's oldest brother. He works as a paramedic on the show, but in real life, Michael is happiest around antique cars.

Blossom's mother may be away in Paris, but Blossom's maternal grandfather stays closer to home. Buzz Richman, played by veteran actor Barnard Hughes, is a traveling jazz pianist who makes frequent visits to the Russo household.

Hughes, who has won both Tony and Emmy awards, starred in the long-running Broadway production of *Da*. His other Broadway credits include *Teahouse of the August Moon, Abelarde and Heloise, Uncle Vanya, The Good Doctor*, and *Prelude to a Kiss*.

Television audiences saw and loved Barnard Hughes in the shows *Lou Grant, Doc, Mr. Merlin*, and *The Cavanaughs*. He was also a regular on two daytime soaps, *The Secret Storm* and *Love of Life*.

Hughes appeared on the big screen in *Oh, God, Maxie, Doc Hollywood*, and *Where's Poppa?*

Along with his actress-wife Helen Sternborg, Hughes splits his time between Los Angeles and New York. The couple have a son, Doug, and a daughter, Laura.

She's not a member of the family—but she might as well be. Six LeMuere spends almost as much time in the Russo home as Blossom does. Played by Jenna von Oy, Six is Blossom's talkative best friend and partner in fun.

A native of Connecticut, Jenna is the oldest of four children. By age five, she had shown off her amazing voice at telethons and local community functions. Shortly after, Jenna made her acting debut as Molly in a regional production of *Annie*.

Jenna has also appeared in many television commercials. She played Darla in Goodspeed Opera's production of *Little Rascals* and Gretel in an off-Broadway production of *The Sound of Music*.

Jenna made her motion picture debut playing Suzanne in the Academy Award-winning movie *Born on the Fourth of July*, which starred hunky Tom Cruise. Lucky girl!

Like many of the other *Blossom* co-stars, Jenna is also multi-talented. Her beautiful voice won her a solo in the "Let It Be Earth Day Everyday" album produced by Earthchild Productions with Earthtrust. She also recently recorded a duet with Ben Taylor, the son of pop singers Carly Simon and James Taylor.

"People always say to me, you should make a record," Jenna says, "but I really don't have time. I'm afraid if I try to smoosh too much in, I'll explode!"

When she's not singing or acting, Jenna enjoys dancing, reading, bicycling, and spending time with her family and friends.

CHAPTER SEVEN

Mayim Off the Set

Considering how much time it takes to act in a series, you might think Mayim has little time for anything else. But somehow, Mayim crowds an incredible amount of interests and activities into her life.

First of all, Mayim spends plenty of time doing schoolwork. Just because Mayim is tutored privately on the set doesn't mean she escapes homework!

Education is very important in her close-knit family, so Mayim stays on top of the books. Her favorite subjects are marine biology and environmental sciences. Right now, Mayim is also studying for her SAT college entrance exams.

Like Blossom, Mayim is a musical prodigy. Her greatest musical love is the piano, but she also plays the trumpet. Mayim enjoys listening to popu-

**Environmentally conscious Mayim
shows off her green friend.**

lar music, and one of her favorite groups is The Violent Femmes.

"I think their lyrics are really cool," Mayim says, "and the lead singer is pretty cute."

When she's not listening to today's music, she reaches for albums from a past era, known as the Big Band years. Mayim likes Big Band leaders Duke Ellington and Artie Shaw.

Mayim enjoys dancing as well. She stopped ballet lessons because they took up too much time, but she still enjoys tap, jazz dancing, and just moving to the sounds of C&C Music Factory.

Mayim finds time to work for social causes she believes in, including animal rights, saving the environment, and the plight of the homeless.

"I do a food drive for the homeless," Mayim says, "usually around the December holidays, which is also the same month as my birthday, so I particularly feel like giving something back then. If there is any charity-publicity thing, I'm glad to do it."

To bring attention to environmental issues, Mayim once hosted an ABC special from Sea World to celebrate Earth Day. She's "adopted" several zoo animals, including a whale, a wolf, and a manatee.

Mayim's love for animals doesn't stop at the zoo. At home, Mayim's menagerie of pets includes a couple of cats and a school of fish.

"I want a rat, but I don't think my mom will let me get one," Mayim says.

She's also done her part in the anti-drug campaign. She once sang the national anthem for

30,000 schoolchildren at a "Just Say No" rally in California.

When the United States needed a representative for the United Nations International School's Program for Better Relations Between People of All Countries, Mayim was chosen.

Mayim tries to spend as much time as she can with her family. Despite her high salary and many responsibilities, Mayim looks to her parents for help.

When Mayim wants to relax, she turns to her paints and canvasses. Most often, Mayim's paintings focus on the environment and the human condition.

She also enjoys playing video games and shopping with her friends.

"On the one hand, I have no trouble speaking with adults about adult things," Mayim says, "but on the other hand, I know it's important to cherish my youth as long as I can."

Mayim hangs out with many of the same friends she has had since kindergarten.

"I know they love me for who I am," she says.

Mayim knows that a lot of people think she's growing up too fast. But she doesn't see it that way.

"I'm enjoying myself," she says. "I'm still a kid. I do things that other kids do."

CHAPTER EIGHT

Mayim and Jenna: Friends Forever

On TV, Blossom and Six are best friends. They share girl talk and secrets, talk about their fave guys, and help each other out of scrapes.

"I think the relationship between Blossom and Six is a very special one," Mayim says. "Boys don't really get together and have sleepovers and really talk the way we do."

In real life, Mayim and Jenna also pal it up. They may not sleep over at each other's houses very often, but they do spend plenty of time together. Their friendship started because the pair thought the show would be better if they really seemed to be at ease with each other. And that meant getting to know each other. But even after their characters had jelled as best friends, Mayim and Jenna continued spending time together. Why? Because they like each other!

Blossom and Six, best friends forever!

The girls also like making jewelry together. That comes in handy for Mayim, who has nine holes in her ears—her lucky number.

When the girls aren't making jewelry, they're out buying it, or, for that matter, buying anything! Mayim and Jenna share a passion for shopping, whether it's at a mall or a funky downtown store. Jenna is always looking for another hat for her collection—she has more than a hundred already.

"If I see a store, I always jump in and find something," Jenna says.

As for Mayim, she's always looking for that special touch that will make an outfit, whether it's a pair of red fishnet stockings or a velvet biker jacket. And she's always looking for another black outfit.

"I like to wear all black and you can't do that on TV," Mayim says.

The only problem with the pair's friendship is that Mayim and Jenna can attract quite a crowd when they go out together. That's especially true if they choose a mall crowded with teenagers!

"When we're both together, people are sure it's us, so we get stared at a lot more," Jenna says.

Neither one of them really minds when their fans stop to say, "Hi." In fact, they're flattered.

"I don't mind the recognition at all," Mayim says. Once, before she was famous, Mayim saw Cyndi Lauper on the street. "It was a major thrill to walk up to her and introduce myself," Mayim recalls.

Another thing the girls have in common is

their love of music. Sometimes when the two are studying together or looking at lines, one of the girls will start humming the words to a song the other is singing. Before they know it, the girls will be singing in harmony. No wonder Blossom and Six are in such close sync once the cameras start rolling!

CHAPTER NINE

Mayim's Future

Mayim is in no hurry to leave *Blossom*. For one thing, she's having too much fun!

The show is also helping Mayim to develop into a full-fledged actress. Because the show features so many great guest stars, Mayim has had a chance to work with such actresses as Phylicia Rashad, who starred in *The Cosby Show*, Rhea Perlman from *Cheers*, and Estelle Getty from *The Golden Girls*.

Mayim says her experience in show business so far has been "overwhelmingly positive."

But no television show lasts forever. Mayim—and her fans—hope *Blossom* will run for many more years. But when it does end, Mayim isn't sure what will come next.

"I'm only 16 and just learning about careers," Mayim says. She "just doesn't know" if she will continue acting once she is grown up.

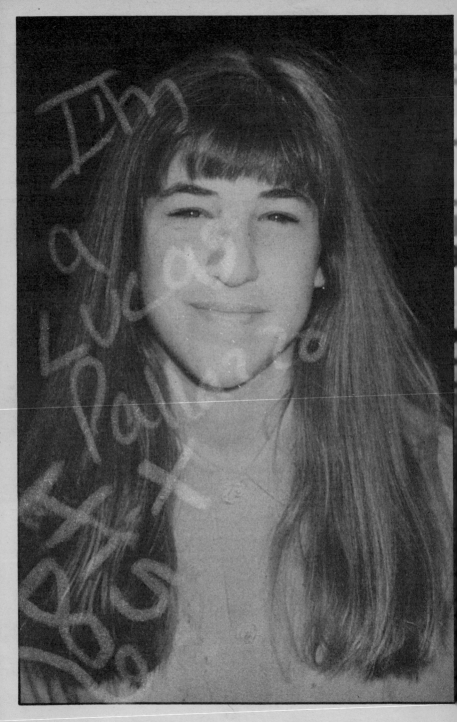

What will she be when she grows up?

"I don't think too far in advance," she says.

Mayim is sure of one thing. No matter what else she does, she will always have a special place in her heart for Blossom, the character and the show.

And we will too!

**Six (Jenna von Oy)
sports her trademark head-wear.**

CHAPTER TEN

The Blossom Gang Speaks Out!

Mayim Bialik on Herself
"I think of myself as an employed actress, not a celebrity."

Joey Lawrence on Dating
"Dating is a totally different thing than seriously going out with someone, like you're one-on-one and you can't see anyone else. I've got a couple of years to wait before I get married."

Jenna von Oy on Hats
"I actually started wearing hats four years ago when I auditioned for *Blossom*. I went in there with a wide-brimmed purple hat, and when they called me back they told me to wear the hat. That became sort of my trademark. Six, my character, wears them.

Mayim Bialik on Life

"I never make any compromises in my life. If there's something I believe in, I say it, even if I turn people off."

Joey Lawrence on his Hometown in Pennsylvania

"Being back there, away from the business, has kept me sane."

Jenna von Oy on People

"I think people need to take a close look at themselves. No matter what age you are, you need to always remember to treat people the same, no matter how much they are different, whether it is by culture, race or religion. Everyone is human. Everyone has feelings."

Mayim Bialik on Getting the Part in *Beaches*

"I really don't know why they picked me. They changed my hair color, they changed the color of my eyes, and they didn't like my singing voice. Beats me."

Joey Lawrence on Making his First Album

"This is something that I've wanted to do for a long time, but TV was just more available to a young kid like myself, so I did that first."

Mayim Bialik on her Parents

"I think a lot of kids feel the need to rebel and say, 'Oooh, I hate my parents.' But I guess I'm different.

My parents and I have always been close. I talk with my mom about basically everything. I respect my parents.''

Beverly Bialik on Mayim's Similarities to Other Teens
''She likes that phone. She worries about what to wear. She worries about her hair. She worries about if she is liked. She's concerned about the other kids.''

Mayim Bialik on *Blossom*
''It's about being your own person.''

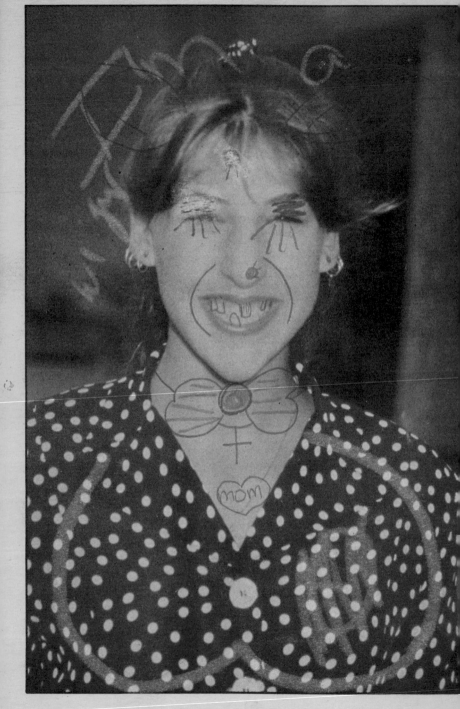

**Mayim Bialik has a lot
to smile about these days!**

CHAPTER ELEVEN

Mayim's Stats and Facts, Faves and Raves

Birthdate: Dec. 12, 1975
Birthplace: San Diego, California
Height: 5'1"
Eyes: Green
Her Name: Mayim means *water* in Hebrew
Parents: Beverly and Barry Bialik
Brother: Isaac, a student at UCLA
Grade: Senior in Los Angeles County High School's Independent Study Program
Favorite Groups: The Sundays, Violent Femmes
Favorite Causes: The environment, animal rights, feminism, the homeless
Favorite Breakfast: Hamburgers. Really!
Musical Instruments: Trumpet, piano, guitar

Athletic Abilities: Dancing, running, swimming, and gymnastics

Adopted Zoo Animals: A whale, a wolf, and a manatee

Favorite Activities: Painting, playing video games, shopping, watching *Beverly Hills, 90210*

Favorite Hunks: Singer Gordon Gano, Jason Priestley, and Luke Perry

Favorite Clothes: Anything black and baggy

Address: Write to Mayim c/o *Blossom*, NBC Studios, 3000 West Alameda Avenue, Burbank, CA., 91253

CHAPTER TWELVE

Totally Awesome Trivia and Puzzles

How much do you really know about Mayim Bialik? Take the Mayim trivia test and find out!

1. **Where did Mayim grow up?**
   A. Manhattan, New York
   B. Los Angeles, California
   C. Miami, Florida
2. **How old was Mayim when she began acting professionally?**
   A. Eleven
   B. Nine
   C. Six
3. **What was the name of the first movie that Mayim ever got a role in?**
   A. *Beaches*
   B. *Pumpkinhead*
   C. *Aliens*

The famous Russo siblings.

4. **Name the character that Mayim played in the hit flick *Beaches*.**
   A. J.J. Hersey
   B. B.J. Flower
   C. C.C. Bloom
5. **How many pierced earring holes does Mayim have in her ears?**
   A. Nine
   B. Two
   C. Seven
6. **Before becoming Blossom, Mayim starred in a short-lived Fox series. What was it called?**
   A. *Married . . . With Children*
   B. *Molloy*
   C. *Sister Kate*
7. **What actress played the adult version of the character Mayim portrayed in *Beaches*?**
   A. Madonna
   B. Demi Moore
   C. Bette Midler
8. **What does Mayim's dad do for a living?**
   A. Television director
   B. Drama coach
   C. Musician
9. **What is Mayim's brother's name?**
   A. Isaac
   B. Jason
   C. Matthew

10. **Which one of these school subjects are among Mayim's favorites?**
A. Marine biology
B. Mathematics
C. Latin

Answers on Page 64

Try your hand at these true/false questions about the whole *Blossom* gang.

1. Jenna von Oy has recorded a duet with Carly Simon's and James Taylor's son, Ben.___T___F
2. Before starring as Nick Russo in *Blossom*, Ted Wass portrayed Danny Dallas on the hit comedy, *Soap*.___T___F
3. Michael Stoyanov, who plays Anthony Russo, has a cat named Cesar.___T___F
4. Jenna von Oy had a bit part in the movie *Beaches*.___T___F
5. Joey Lawrence is a C student in school.___T___F
6. Mayim's name means *water* in Hebrew.___T___F
7. Joey Lawrence has his hair styled before every show by a professional stylist.___T___F
8. The *Blossom* cast is making an album together.___T___F
9. Joey Lawrence loves to collect model cars almost as much as he likes to play keyboards.___T___F
10. Both Mayim and Jenna love to shop.___T___F

Answers on page 64

Fill in the blanks in this fun trivia test about *Blossom*.

1. Blossom's first serious boyfriend was _____.

2. The *Blossom* theme song, "My Opinionation" is performed by _____.

3. Blossom's big brother Anthony works as a _____.

4. When Blossom needed advice from a mother, she dreamed up Claire Huxtable from NBC's _____.

5. Talk show host _____ appeared in one sequence to tell Blossom about world affairs.

6. Television alien _____ helped Blossom out when she needed advice about boys.

7. The *Blossom* crew donned "*Blossom* World Tour" T-shirts in one episode and spoofed the *Truth or Dare* movie by _____.

8. On one episode, Six gets jealous because she thinks Blossom is spending too much time with _____.

9. Joey's first on-screen kiss came when he fell for a teen named _____, who didn't speak any English.

10. Blossom wears an average of _____ outfits on every episode.

Answers on Page 64

GET CROSSED WITH *BLOSSOM*

Across

1. What is Blossom's grandfather's first name?
2. What state is *Blossom* filmed in?
3. Blossom's father makes his living playing _____.
4. What European city is Blossom's mother living in?
5. Name an instrument that both Mayim and Blossom play.

Down

1. What musical group dances with Blossom and Six after the pair sleep outside a concert hall to try to get tickets to their show?
2. What is Blossom's last name?
3. What is Blossom's first boyfriend's name?
4. Who's Blossom's best friend?

Answers on Page 64

GET CROSSED WITH *BLOSSOM*

The *Blossom* bunch!

THE OUTRAGEOUS OUTFIT SEARCH

Try to find the names of the clothes hidden in the puzzle below that are part of a typical Blossom outfit. The words can go up, down, forward, backward, or diagonally.

Hat
Leggings
Vest
Overalls
Suspenders
Tights
Socks
Shirt

```
S  G  N  I  G  G  E  L  E  V
V  U  T  E  O  W  T  E  E  Q
T  V  S  T  G  D  V  A  R  L
S  H  I  P  V  B  V  A  H  O
H  B  O  V  E  R  A  L  L  S
I  C  B  R  S  N  T  U  X  S
R  T  A  B  T  C  D  A  F  K
T  E  R  I  S  G  I  E  S  C
L  S  T  H  G  I  T  H  R  O
B  O  T  T  E  V  E  R  T  S
```

Answers on page 64

ANSWER KEY:

Multiple choice:
1) B 2)A 3)B 4)C 5)A 6)B 7)C 8)B 9)A 10)A

True/False:
1)T 2)T 3)F 4)F 5)F 6)T 7)F 8)F 9)T 10)T

Fill in the blanks:

1) Vinnie	6) Alf
2) Dr. John	7) Madonna
3) paramedic	8) Vinnie
4) *The Cosby Show*	9) Anna
5) Phil Donahue	10) Six

Get Crossed With *Blossom*:

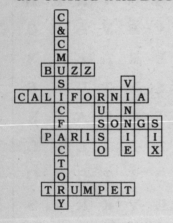

The Outrageous Outfit Search:

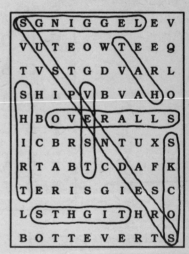